Embracing *Your* Story

How to Build a **Great Life** Out of Hardships

ALISA SMEDLEY

First Printing October 2020

ISBN 978-1-953755-00-1 (paperback)

1. Self-help. 2. Motivational and Inspirational. 3. Personal Growth 4. Success

Smedley, Alisa

Embracing Your Story: How to Build a Great Life Out of Hardship

Book cover design by Kimb Manson Graphic Design

Interior Designer Jordan Hughes

Library of Congress Control Number: 2020917868

DEDICATION

This book is dedicated to my sister Shelly and my brother Micheal. One helps me to heal from the darkness of our childhood and the other keeps me thinking about the possibilities of the future. I love you both - all we've ever had was each other.

"No matter how hopeless things seemed...I just always kept dreaming."

Alisa Smedley

TABLE OF CONTENTS

ACKNOWLEDGMENTS

This book would not have happened without the support of a few important people, places, and playgrounds in my life.

The permanent members of my Village – Charon, Sharon, Shiryl and Darlene - without your unconditional love and support I would not be who I am today. You each make me a better woman and parent.

TeAndre, thank you for reading and enjoying this project from the very beginning. You told me that my story would help people.

To two of my mentors, Lucius and Phyllis, I thank you both for helping me to hold it together when life got difficult.

Alice, you polished my words. Thank you for embracing this project.

Takoma Park, Montgomery County, Maryland, USA - the first place that provided me with peace and opportunity.

Finally, a special thanks to Cuyahoga Community College in Cleveland, Ohio. The hope and education that you gave my mother in the mid-1970's changed our lives. Tri-C remained a safe space for the rest of her life.

FOREWORD

My name is Lucius Lewis and Alisa Smedley is both a ment[...] and friend. I have watched her grow over the past 30 year[...] Lisa has a rare combination of drive and determination, whi[...] having the compassion to help others. She is very focuse[...] and determined to produce results. As I have watched h[...] over the years, it has been a delight to see her person[...] motivation reach new levels. This book will provide valuab[...] lessons about how any of us can overcome the tough times[...]

It has been very interesting to watch Lisa's journey! N[...] matter what the circumstances, she always pressed on. Sh[...] has certainly been an inspiration to me and has helped me [...] grow in so many areas myself.

Embracing Your Story will share the deeply personal an[...] sometimes painful stories from her life. You will hear abou[...] the spiritual and educational foundation that Lisa receive[...] from her mother, and the creativity and entrepreneurshi[...] learned from her father.

Through it all, Lisa has managed to stay humble an[...] grounded. I could go on and on about Lisa and what sh[...] means to me! I just want to be there to provide assistanc[...] to her in any way that I can. I also want to remind her tha[...] there is no limit to the heights that she can reach. May yo[...]

enjoy getting to know Alisa Smedley as I have over the years. I challenge you to embrace your own story in the end.

Lucius Lewis

Better Way Institute

INTRODUCTION

Each of us has a story to tell. In this book I will share ten important scenes from my life. Some are sad or funny, while others are hopeful or hopeless. I am always brutally honest and will show the connection between those situations that we are born into, those that we choose and how they all come together to shape us. One definition of *embrace* is to accept completely. I used to distance myself from my past. Once I learned to embrace my story, my life honestly took a new direction. I thank you for joining me on this journey!

I was formed and prepared for life by my past. I have survived the worst of it. An amazing thing happens when you overcome a tough season...you get stronger, more confident, better able to handle the next tough season. My hardships, my scars, and my stories have made me strong.

I wrote this book to share how experiences, even the difficult ones, can be used to help us build better lives. It takes hard work and often many, many years...but it is possible to build a great life out of difficult beginnings. Once you escape the hurt and learn the lessons, it is then that you can go for it. With the right plan, the next chapter of your life can be great! I am a witness.

My hope with *Embracing Your Story* is that you will find a blueprint to follow if you have had a difficult life. The stories shared here are real. Each chapter of the book offers some wisdom. After each story I share *Lessons Learned* and ask a few key questions about your situation. I hope that you can find answers to your situation within these pages. Join me as I discuss practical strategies for building a great life out of our hardships. Consider this book as a tool - a how-to guide, a journal, and a workbook all in one. I also encourage you to discover your own stories.

Alisa Smedley

My Story

CHAPTER 1

Minus 20

On the number line of life, I was born on -20. Let me explain something about the number line and a thing called the American Dream. Imagine a number line. It has a starting point, or zero, at the center. If you move to either side of the number line you land on different points. One direction represents positive numbers, while the other direction represents negative numbers. These points tell a lot about the kind of life that you will have.

Speaking of life, let's look at the American Dream. It is a common phrase that gives us hope. It hints at the possibilities of a better tomorrow. Opportunities that, in America we are told, are our right. Those of us who live in the United States enjoy a freedom and wealth that does not exist in most of the world. This is why our borders are tested daily by those desperate to get in! For me, the American Dream is all about potential. You can improve your personal circumstance if you decide to -- no matter where your story begins. In this country you can reach your potential if you fully understand the American Dream.

Let me paint two pictures of the Dream. For those who are born at zero, they will have a childhood filled with adequate clothing, food, doctor appointments, and caring parents. The child completes elementary school and maybe even has an adult who makes time to read to them at bedtime. The years go by and around age 16 they get their learner's permit to drive a car. By 18 they may have their own car to drive themselves to the high school where they will undoubtedly graduate. The next step is college, where they will obtain a degree, meet their future spouse, and marry. A good post-graduation job is waiting for them and a house is soon purchased. Kids and graduate school may happen next and inevitably a bigger house is purchased. A hefty 401(k) or pension quietly secures a comfortable retirement. Life is good.

For those of us born on the *other* side of the number line, there is a very different story taking place. Our future is not as certain; our early years are not as secure. A child on the negative side of the line will likely live with one parent, in older housing that will probably cause lead poisoning and asthma. They will attend substandard schools, eventually lose interest and drop out. They may begin to have children of their own and be forced to take a dead end, low-paying job to support their fragile family. Life on the negative side of the line is a series of failures and disappointments! You hear about the American Dream, you may even know a family that is close to living it. Somehow, though, you cannot seem to find the door that leads into a more rewarding and stable life.

Stress, pressure, and shut-off notices become a regular part of your life, like familiar "friends" that drop by. They may lead to cigarettes, obesity and lottery tickets as you try to cope. Life on the negative side of the number line is hard.

I was born on the negative side of the number line. Not only did I not begin life at zero, but rather, I started at *-20*.

I literally have 20 barriers that I was BORN INTO!! I had teenage parents (15 and 17), both were sexually abused as children, and I never had access to sufficient food or health care. Alcoholism and addiction ran through my bloodline. I also have a mild learning disability called *dyspraxia* that went undiagnosed until my thirties. We lived on welfare my entire childhood and my father went to prison when I was ten.

The list of barriers goes on, but my point is that many of us are born on the wrong side of that great number line of life. That American Dream is more like a nightmare that we cannot seem to wake up from. In our story, everything is hard, everything takes so long, and everything is a struggle. On top of being *born* into a negative, I made bad choices, too, that caused me to move further to the left, and further in the wrong direction.

The number line determines what it will take to be successful. We can all be successful! We all have potential. The key is to understand *where you are* on the number line.

Once you understand where you are, you can learn how to maximize the assets that you have and minimize the effects of destructive or dysfunctional components of your story.

I first understood the concept of the <u>number line</u> in my early twenties. I was 23 and managing a retail store. I hired a young white kid who worked for a few hours after school. He was 16 and I taught him everything he needed to be a good clerk. Two years later when he was a senior about to graduate from high school, he and some buddies went to Myrtle Beach for spring break. He was so excited when he got back to work! I remember him showing me his pictures and telling me about the great time he had. I had never been to the beach and enjoyed sharing his experience. I thought of him as a kid brother and was so proud of him. I felt proud, too, that as a good manager, I was preparing him for the world of work.

My young worker went straight to college after graduation, along with his high school girlfriend. Each summer he would come back to the store and work until the fall semester began. Over the years he became a seasoned worker and a valuable member of my team.

I will never forget one summer I was running the store with no assistant manager. Although human resources was running ads and even had a few interviews, we just did not find any good candidates. As our busiest season of the year was approaching, I came down with a bad case of bronchitis. We were waiting for a huge shipment, over 500 cases of merchandise, and I was at home very sick. I called the store daily to see if the shipment had arrived, and told my clerks to let me know and I'd come in to help unpack. A few days passed and no shipment. When I returned to work I found out that the shipment *had* arrived and this young man told the crew not to call me. He knew I would drag myself in to help, despite being in no condition to do so. Instead he convinced other crew members to push and get the delivery unpacked and on the shelves. I learned that day that I had created an environment of loyalty and love among those workers. We were like family at my store. That team and our accomplishments remains one of my proudest moments.

This young man and his girlfriend soon married and began a family. After he graduated college, he came back to our company in a position downtown at our headquarters.

We stayed close over the years. At age 24, he was married to a nurse, was a homeowner, and had earned a bachelor's degree; while I was age 31, living in an apartment, did not own a car, and had to drop out of college to care for a family member. Although I was older, and had met him as a part-time worker, he now was more successful than I was. I was still helping customers and ringing on a cash register (a job); while this young man was well on his way in a *career*. I pondered how he had passed me by, in terms of life accomplishments.

I did not blame him. I loved this young man. I just took a closer look at how the American Dream works for some of us, but not the same way for all of us.

I began to understand that *how* it works has a lot to do with where you start. That is when it hit me…the number line. He began on the positive side of the number line while I began on the negative side. His path to success was many steps closer than my own. Age did not matter. He had advantages over me due to where he started on the number line.

When you are born on the negative side of the number line, it may take longer to access the American Dream, but it is not impossible. Sometimes it takes years longer, but fortunately, you <u>can</u> reach the other side of the number line. In reality, it may take a lifetime to reach the positive side of the line. When you already start out on the negative side of the number line, there is little room for error, you simply do not have any time to waste. Remember that!

I am very grateful to have met and shared a relationship with this young man. For my birthday one year he gave me a communicator, just like what the crew of the Starship Enterprise wore on *Star Trek,* because he knew I was a huge fan. He had gone to a Star Trek convention and bought it for me. We were unlikely friends; but held a mutual respect, admiration and love for one another. We talked openly about race and discrimination. He gained a sensitivity about how minorities and women are often treated and mistreated. I gained an understanding that the number line existed and must be understood in order to make progress in life.

Lessons Learned

In every chapter I will review what I learned from the story. These key points will illustrate how to pull out the life lesson from every experience that you encounter. We must understand life's lessons in order to reach our full potential, to build and become our best self.

From the events in the story *Minus 20* here is what I learned:

It is important to take an honest look at our past, our "story"

After I realized that a number line existed, I could recall my life – how my childhood and early adulthood led me to my situation in *Minus 20.* Instead of being mad that other people were more successful than I was, I chose to examine myself. It is important to be able to look at yourself and to be honest with yourself. You will never grow if you cannot take an honest look within. Acknowledging my story empowered me. I realized that I held the power to get my life together! Nobody else…just me. When you mature enough to realize that it's not the man, or the system, or your family that is keeping you down, you can begin to make choices that can improve your life. You truly have the <u>power</u> to start improving your life immediately. The power lies within each decision that you make. As long as there is life there is hope. You must, however, be real with yourself.

Be someone who can truly celebrate the success of others

Learn how to be happy for other people. Never let the green-eyed monster of jealousy or envy enter the picture. Be happy for others – your turn will come if you do what you are supposed to do. It is important not to measure your life by comparing yourself to others. There will always be those who have more and those who have less than you. Be content with what you have. And if you are not content, what do you need to do to get what you want? In this case, it's all about you. While you chase your dream, enable yourself to join others and celebrate their dream. Be sure to be sincere, you do not grow if you are fake!

Mentor others in order to solidify your own talents and beliefs

When you help someone else, you become a part of their success. It takes nothing away from you when you contribute to someone else's growth and development. I have heard foolish people say, "don't teach him so much, he may take your job." My response has always been that when someone takes my job, God has an even bigger job waiting for me! Nobody can take what God has planned for you. You will reach your destiny sooner if you help others reach theirs. Mentoring and coaching others will always pay off, whether directly or indirectly.

Take responsibility for the role you played in where you are today

Much of the time, where we are in life is due to personal actions, choices, and decisions. In other words, when things are not working it could be because we simply messed up and made a bad choice, or a bunch of bad choices. Other times life just happens. In that case, we must decide how we will react to the curveballs that life may throw at us. Be brave, face the future and take action.

Spend time thinking about where you want to go in life...and then, do something!

After you examine where you are on the number line, can be excited for someone else's success, have found someone to mentor, and take responsibility for your own role in past failures, the only thing left is to get busy. Get busy doing something, taking action steps – big and small. Everyday take a step or steps toward your destiny. Winners are not lazy and they do not procrastinate either.

Questions to Think About

Everyone who knows me knows that I have a gift for asking questions. There are times when we must ask ourselves some tough questions in order to move our lives forward. In each chapter I will ask a few questions to get you thinking. I suggest that you use these questions to start a journal. You can write your thoughts in a book, or use technology (your tablet, phone, or computer) to capture your thoughts. Try to truly reflect on your answers to the questions. The goal is to help you grow.

- Were you born on the positive or negative side of the number line? Explain.

- Where do you want to be on the number line of life next year? In five years? Ten years?

- Describe what your life looks like in the future. Think about what you need to do to reach these goals? Be detailed.

Final Thoughts

In this chapter I shared how I discovered the number line and its relationship to the American Dream. It is such an important concept; it literally helped me to better understand my life, my struggles, and my destiny. Once you understand how the game works, you can start to learn the rules and eventually put yourself in a position to win.

I jumped right in with my story about the number line. I want to go back to the beginning when I was child. Embracing your story requires you to look back to your childhood. Some of what is going on with you today, started way back when. The next chapters share nine more stories from my childhood. Let's take a peek at my early years in Cleveland, Ohio.

CHAPTER 2

Reading the Sports Page

I was born on E. 80th Street off of Woodland Avenue in Cleveland, Ohio, on the southeast side. My parents were both teenagers (15 and 17-years-old). My mother had been kicked out of East Tech High School when the school discovered that she was pregnant with me. Society did not tolerate teenage pregnancy back in the day. She had to be quickly removed from among the good girls before she could be a bad influence on them. My street was a short street, with a cemetery at one end and a dead end alley at the other. Such depressing surroundings led my grandparents to move further east, to a street off of Kinsman Avenue, when I was almost 3 years-old.

Shortly after moving in, we learned that my mother was having another baby, pregnant this time by a different man (my sister's father). As a young, unmarried, and soon to be mother of two kids, my mother was embarrassed and full of shame. She was 19-years-old and uncertain about how our future would look. She had to do something! Finishing high school became a major goal for her.

So while my mother made her way to classes at the Adult Education Center every day, I was left in the care of my grandfather. He didn't know much about kids, but he did his best with me. He took me everywhere. When he had to go pick up lumber or bags of concrete, I was right there with him. He would explain what materials he was buying, and what project it was for. When my grandfather was young, he was a construction worker. He was retired by the time that I came along, so now his time was occupied with special projects around the house. Truthfully, I think he just wanted to keep busy.

I was his little apprentice. He would walk me through the plans, tell me how long the project should take us – "we'll probably finish up before the fall," he would say. I helped my grandfather build the back porch and seal the driveway with blacktop. I even wanted to assist with the roof repairs, but my grandmother would not hear of it. Grandpa was always working – cutting the grass, painting the garage, or fixing stuff. Being right at his side is where I learned my own solid work ethic.

When we were not roaming the city looking for building supplies, we sat at the kitchen table and he read to me. As I got older he taught me my letters and eventually I practiced reading to him. I mastered reading using the sports page of the *Cleveland Plain Dealer*. Due to my grandfather, I walked into kindergarten reading at a 3rd grade level. Many years later, after he developed Alzheimer's disease, I sat at that same kitchen table and read to him.

Reading the sports page with my grandfather was a daily ritual. As a huge fan of the game, my grandfather used baseball to teach me many things. I knew every player – Buddy Bell, Rico Carty, Dennis Eckersley, and Rick Manning -- all were names that I grew up on while reading the sports page with my grandfather. On Saturday afternoons we would watch the Cleveland Indians games on the T.V. or listen to away games on the radio. Our times together, reading the sports page, connected us. He shared the game that he loved with the grandchild that he adored.

My grandfather was a simple man. For someone with only a high school education, he knew an awful lot about the world. He had lived through a national depression and several wars. He was very careful with money and had purchased three homes on a modest income.

My grandfather talked to me about what life was like while different presidents were in office. He admired Harry Truman, even if Truman did have to make the awful decision to drop an atomic bomb on the Japanese. He believed that Truman was just a regular guy – not a "fancy pants" like some of the other politicians. I get my love of history from him.

My dear grandfather gave me a wonderful gift – time. He would spend hours listening to my silly talk, answering at least a million questions from my curious little mind, and telling me repeatedly that I could do anything. And he really believed that I could. Quality time with my grandfather gave me a confidence that I still carry within me. I think that all children need someone to spend time with them, not bound by busy schedules or demanding jobs. A caring adult who can devote calm hours to a child's education and development creates children who are whole.

From the events in the story *Reading the Sports Page* here is what I learned:

Lessons Learned

Make home a solid foundation for your children, a place to build good lives

Home should provide each member with the tools needed for a quality life. We must be strategic with how our home operate. It also means thinking about things like cleanliness safety, nutrition, education, etc. Our family unit may take on many different forms these days, but regardless of who makes up the family, we should always think about what the members of the family need. If you have children, this responsibility becomes even more important. You do no need to live in a mansion to have a solid foundation! Love emotional support, adequate financial support, and a peacefu environment are a strong foundation for building good lives

Be devoted to your children

If you decide to have children you must be devoted to their care. Make choices and decisions that put your children's needs first! The early years require a great deal of effort and energy, but your children will not be young forever. You must understand that you can do great deal of damage in those early years if you mess it up. Even if your parenting circumstances are not the best, decide to do your best with what you have.

The story *Reading the Sports Page* is about beginnings. Even if your family does not have as many resources as another family, you must learn how to assess what you do have and do the most with it. You CAN make something good happen.

Develop your children's skills at an early age – you are their first teacher. Preparing your children for school begins at HOME

Children can be prepared for academic success very early on. Read to your babies! Everywhere you go can become a classroom. While standing at the bus stop, have your little ones count how many blue cars they see. At the grocery store have them look for shapes. At the park encourage them to name and describe the animals or plants that they see. It is not difficult to prepare your child for success at school even if you do not have the highest education. All subjects – math, reading, science, all begin with very simple concepts that we can learn as children. The main thing is to show your children that you are excited about learning. Teach them to be curious about their world. You can improve your skills right along with your kids! It only requires patience, vision, creativity, and an adult who is willing to invest in their little people. Remember that they watch everything that you do. Show them that learning is important to you.

Select your caregivers with care! Easy and convenient is not always SAFE

As a parent or guardian it is your responsibility to keep your children safe. Deciding who will care for your children in your absence is very important. It may cost you a little time, money, or effort, but finding the best person or situation to watch your children is absolutely critical.

You must understand the difference between people who educate children and those people who "watch kids." A formal daycare setting does not necessarily mean that any learning is going on. The other side of that coin is that a private home with a licensed provider may be more professional and organized than a center. Spend time selecting the best environment for your little ones. Look for examples of what the kids are learning. Television watching should be absent or very limited. Young children's brains are still forming and they need activities that promote creativity and thinking.

Another thing, take into account who will have access to your children. Look closely at who works at the center in addition to teaching staff. In a private home setting, consider family members, friends, and others who may drop by during the day. In other words – watch everybody. Listen to your children. As they tell you about their day and they mention an unfamiliar name, ask questions.

Questions to Think About

- How do you feel about learning? Did you like school?

- Have you done your very best in selecting caregiver(s) for your child or children?

- Did you take the time to research the facility or provider?

- Can you live with the consequences of a poor decision?

Final Thoughts

I truly believe that we can do the impossible if we have at least one person in our lives who thinks that we can. My grandfather believed in me and nurtured me in ways that rose above our financial situation. He was my first cheerleader -- always encouraging, teaching, and supporting me!

One important lesson that came from this relationship is that we should recognize the people who make "deposits" into our lives. Who loved you unconditionally when you were young? Who listened to you? I can always tell an adult who was not heard as a child – they monopolize the conversation and must always be the center of attention. If you had no one in your early years, consider how you can be that person for a child in your life now. Consider volunteering as a mentor.

We all have a responsibility to care for the children around us. That includes our households and our community at large. Educating children as early as possible and keeping them safe is a wise investment. In the next chapter I share what happened when I started school.

CHAPTER 3

School

The day came when my grandfather would no longer babysit me – instead, every morning he would deliver me to the Andrew J. Rickoff school building. I now became exposed to people outside of my home.

I loved learning and walked into kindergarten reading at a 3rd grade level. I caught on pretty quickly that I was different from the other kids. The first few years were fine and the differences were barely noticeable – kindergarten to 3rd grade were wonderful times with teachers that sparked my creativity, who really got to know me, and invested heavily in my education. I have never forgotten those elementary school teachers.

My kindergarten teacher, Mrs. Holloway, played the piano and taught us to enjoy every corner of the classroom. The play areas and learning centers were colorful and so inviting. First grade with Mrs. Grant taught me to sit still and become a serious student. She was preparing our young minds for success, as she explained to us every day. Mrs. Heath, my second grade teacher, snacked on apples while she read to us in the afternoons – that was my favorite time of the day. She was fun - her voice was rich with animation and her eyes sparkled.

Young Miss Haynesworth got married during our 3rd grade year. It was a year of excitement because she was a new teacher, just out of college. We read the newspaper in class. In one assignment that she gave us, we tracked the prices for basic grocery items during the entire school year. We learned how prices went up or down, depending on the season. We learned how to make a grocery list for when we went shopping with our families. I never shared with her that my family lived on food stamps. Instead of green dollars, my family used white paper sheets, called food coupons that we tore from little booklets to buy our groceries. By the end of the month there was very little food or coupons left. "At least I'm learning the skill," I thought to myself. "Someday I will have money to use shopping lists and plan my meals so that we can eat right. Someday, when I grow up…it won't be so hard," I reminded myself.

Fourth grade is when everything really changed. That was the year that I began to feel poor. It was a tough year all around. My father committed a horrible crime and was sentenced to prison. I did not get to see him very much even before he was locked up, but his brothers, my uncles, made up for his neglect. They lived near me and I saw them all of the time. My dad's crime made front page news for months. He killed a man. The whole incident was painful, embarrassing, and very public.

During this family crisis, fourth grade began in September and we received our school supply lists. As I read the list I felt that sinking feeling in my stomach -- the one that I always got when I knew we didn't have enough money for something. I waited a few days before giving my mother the list. Depending on how she was feeling, I knew that handing her that piece of paper could spark sadness or rage. Or both. Luckily, my sister was in 1ˢᵗ grade and did not need many supplies. But my list was long…two columns of stuff that we couldn't afford. I hated shopping for school supplies. We would go to the store and my mother would go over our lists, trying to budget the little money that we had.

We never got everything on our lists. "We barely have enough money to buy school clothes, let alone glue, six notebooks, and folders, too," my mother would remind me. After a few weeks we were expected to have everything from the list at school and in our desk. If the teacher asked us to pull out an item that I didn't have, I would lie and say that I forgot it at home that day. And the teacher would start to lecture me about needing to be more responsible and wishing that I would come to school prepared. I accepted those tongue lashings because I was not going to let this teacher know that my family could not afford the scissors, or compass, or the correct lined paper. In my head I'm thinking, we are in survival mode, lady, the heck with "college-ruled" paper. We bought the paper that was on sale at Kmart!

As we got further into the school year, things were starting to settle down. I was in the highest reading group and one week it was my turn to be the group leader. As group leader you had to review the chapter with your group, prepare an activity, and provide a treat. As honors students, the curriculum was preparing us for success in college and in our careers. I tried to learn all that I could, always thinking that if I could just work hard, and do well in school, I could have a better life someday. For my turn as group leader I was ready! I planned a fun activity and successfully begged my mother to buy a little bag of candy treats with her food stamps. I had practiced "teaching" the lesson at home in the mirror for hours. I barely slept the night before I was to give the reading group lesson. I got up early that morning, and headed off to school. It was also Open House that day. I had forgotten about that and began to feel a little nervous. My mother was never able to come to open house because she was in school herself.

As I arrived in our classroom I saw a few parents there. I waved at my friend's mom and dad. I knew them because they lived on the same street as my family. The teacher then walks over to me and says that she would like to speak to me. She led me over by her desk and asked if I wouldn't mind giving my lesson to my friend, the girl from my street, because her parents were there today. "We both know that your parents aren't coming," she added. I felt a lump swelling in my throat and fought off the tears. *"Never let them see you cry, you come home and cry, but NEVER let-them-see-you-cry-in-public,"* I could hear my mother's voice inside my head, repeating over and over the message that had been drilled in me for years.

I gave everything to my friend – the game, the candy treats, all of it -- and took a seat in the reading group, only NOT in the leader's seat in front. I sat there in the circle of the reading group feeling numb, just trying to hold it together, get out of school, and make it home.

That day I learned that teachers play politics and that school is not always a fair system. I had no grown-up to join me or to represent me inside this environment, my school. I was all alone in this place. I learned that no matter how hard I worked, or how much I tried to come to school prepared some teachers would not understand my struggles. The reality was that my parents were young, and too busy with their own problems – one was trying to earn a GED and the other was locked up in prison. I was on my own. Only time would eventually allow me to escape and build the kind of life that I dreamed about.

I made it through that day and the remainder of the school year. However, school was never the same for me. Fourth grade made my inner light a little dimmer. I was happy when school let out in June. I had researched the top 50 books that kids going to college should read -- considered classics -- and planned my own reading list. I was looking forward to a great summer, but that's another story.

From the events in the story *School* here is what I learned:

Lessons Learned

Get in the game

If possible, become active at your child's school. Volunteer to participate in classroom activities. If you do not have kids of your own, then substitute children who matter to you - nieces, nephews, grandchildren, godchildren, etc. Teachers cannot do all of the work. Teachers and families are partners in the educational process. Being visible is important.

Understand the politics

Education is very political on many levels. Parents need to understand how the system works and get involved. Get to know both the teachers and administration at the school. Attend parent meetings so that your voice is heard. Clearly communicate expectations and goals for your child's progress. You should also offer to help. *"I want Kevin to do well in math this year. How can I help him at home?"* Your child will be treated better at school if everyone knows that at least one adult is actively involved!

Monitor the affects of finances on your children

Every school year I felt stress in the month of August because most times we were unprepared to buy school supplies. My mother was overwhelmed and verbalized her frustration with us kids. Remember that children take their cues from you. I suggest having open conversations about money, but try to frame it as a lesson, a teachable moment.

Plant positive seeds in your kids' minds: *"We can't buy that right now, but if we start to save our money we can buy it in the spring."* Try to encourage good money habits like saving, setting financial goals, and comparing prices before you buy something. Take advantage of lay-away if stores offer it. This will teach your children two valuable skills – planning and patience.

Remember that life is seasonal

Another lesson that I learned from this time is that life is seasonal. The early years of my school experience were glorious and unforgettable. Then I hit a rough patch on the road to my education. I adjusted, and hung on until I found another caring teacher who inspired me a few grades later.

You will have some great school years and some challenging ones. The key is to figure out early in the school year which type of year it will be. When I became a parent, one year my daughter had a teacher who I felt was prejudiced. I got this feeling after a few conversations and a visit to her classroom to observe. Once I figured out the situation, I enrolled my daughter with a licensed tutoring center for the rest of the school year. I figured that any "damage" that this one teacher could cause would be countered by the support that my child would get from the tutor. My plan worked. When the teacher made derogatory comments about my daughter on a report card, I was able to provide a statement from her tutor and requested that it be included in her record. There is more than one way to skin a cat. I could only afford the private tutoring for that one school year, but I knew that it was necessary if my suspicions were correct.

School is not the only experience that is seasonal. We go through seasons at home, on our jobs, even at church. Understand the season and plan accordingly.

Questions to Think About

- Are you in contact with your child's teachers and administration? Do you support activities at your child's school? Time and money are both valuable.

- Have you shared your goals for your child's progress with the teachers?

- How do you predict how your child's school year will turn out?

- Are your children learning positive or negative lessons about your family finances?

Final Thoughts

This chapter recounted pleasant memories of my early education. It also reminded me of the time when school became unpleasant. This truth is the cause for many students of color to drop out of school. We must find ways to keep our children interested in learning. Learning to navigate our way through the educational system is critical for all parents.

I believe that we have the power to find nuggets of good in any situation if we train ourselves to look hard. Poor families are generally very good at getting to the bottom line. We learn early how to recognize who will be helpful and who will not. Reading people and situations is a skill to cultivate. Accepting the realities of our situation is an opportunity to put a plan in place. Never forget that you have the power to counter any obstacles that others try to put in your way. By making a few strategic moves, you can position yourself and your children for success.

The next chapter describes a time when school is out and during the summer vacation I encounter the neighborhood bully.

CHAPTER 4

Summertime

Corner stores are found everywhere in Cleveland. Our store was located at the corner of Bartlett and E. 149th Street. We had moved into a large two-family house that my grandparents owned. My grandparents lived downstairs and my mother, my little sister and I lived upstairs. We had a huge backyard and would spend hours outside playing kickball, baseball, and climbing trees. There was always something fun to do to pass the hours on warm summer days.

The summer after my father went to prison is one that I will never forget. An older boy moved into the neighborhood, he was the cousin of a girl who was in my class at school. My fun-filled summer suddenly got complicated when he started noticing me. For some reason, that I have never understood, this 16-year-old boy hated me. I was eleven and had never spoken one word to this boy. It started with evil looks as he rode his bike past my front porch. A few weeks into the summer he stopped in front of my house and threatened to beat me up if I came off of the porch.

My mind was swirling. Growing up as a kid in the hood you learn to process information quickly. I looked down the street in the direction of our corner store. Our house was about 20 or 25 houses from the corner. I thought about how long I could avoid leaving my yard, when a thought jumped to the front of my brain. Kools cigarettes. My mother's brand was Kools. I thought about how to reduce my trips to the store to buy her cigarettes. She was unlikely to stop smoking that summer -- not only was she *not* going to quit smoking, but lately she was under a lot of stress which meant that she was smoking even more. This is important because I was her courier to walk to the store and replace her packs of cigarettes. Thank God that society has since realized that maybe children shouldn't be able to purchase cigarettes. My life was being threatened but I knew that I could not stand between my mother and her addiction. I would need to leave my porch to make a cigarette run. It was inevitable.

The threats and menacing stares went on for about 2 weeks. When I had to, I would run to the store as fast as I could, make my purchase and run back to my house. The fear of him "catching" me was growing into a knot in my stomach. I couldn't tell my mother. She had enough to worry about. The boy started telling other kids on our street what he was going to do to me.

One day I was sitting on the porch reading and he rode by my house. A few minutes later, he rode past again, stopped his bike, sat there and looked at me. I very calmly closed my book, being careful to put a bookmark inside so I wouldn't lose my page. I walked down the concrete steps and walked right up to him. I told him I wasn't scared of him, I was going to leave my porch whenever I felt like it this summer, and was prepared to defend my right to do so.

A twisted grin came over his face and he threw his bike down. He started moving around me in a circle, sizing me up. I put my fists up. I said, "you might be bigger than me, and stronger than me, but you ain't going to stop me. I'm not afraid of you." Then he punched me in the eye so hard that it knocked me down. The fight was on! We wrestled around on the ground, while I am biting and kicking and scratching him. I felt like I was fighting for my life. He was so big and heavy, I struggled to push him off of me.

My little sister was playing with her dolls in the backyard when she heard all of the commotion. She ran down the driveway toward the street and saw us fighting on the front lawn. She yelled at him to get off of me and then took off running toward the door. She was going to get our mother! I knew what was about to happen now....the cavalry was on the way! If I could hold on a few more minutes, the tide would turn in my favor.

My mother ran up on him and kicked him off of me. "You my size!" she yelled at him (along with a few colorful words that I won't repeat now). He got up on his feet and she punched him in the mouth. My mother was 27-years-old, tall and tough as nails. She was in a gang when she was younger and only motherhood had softened her heart. This boy was about to learn a lesson that I had always known — my mother loved her kids! She would die for us.

She helped me stand up and both of us defended ourselves, collectively stomping and kicking him! By now people were on their porches watching the drama. All of a sudden some of the older men on the street came over and broke up the fight. I wondered where they had been when this mess first got started.

The sun went down that warm evening and my eye began to swell. My first black eye. We cried and hugged each other —my mother, my little sister and me. Once again we had to show the world that we would not be victims. We stuck together and fought together when necessary. That's what love looks like when you live in constant hardship. A young single mother, with two little girls, who was just trying to survive. This incident would not be the last time that we had to defend our little family in a big, mean world. But nobody else on that street messed with us after that! Including the troubled young man who attacked me. He went on to be incarcerated the following summer – he beat a boy to death.

From the events in the story *Summertime* here is what I learned:

Lessons Learned

Learn how to recognize a bully

As I mentioned I had never spoken one word to the young man in this story. He made a decision to try to bully me for reasons known only to him. I learned that we must learn how to spot the bully and how to respond when bullied. When people try to intimidate, threaten, or harass us, we must face it quickly. The situation will only get worse with time.

Face what you fear

The young man was shocked when I walked up to him. He was expecting me to live in fear for the entire summer. I decided that I would enjoy my summer at whatever the cost. If you face a similar situation try to find someone to tell. Also, try adjusting your response to the bully. They love the smell of fear and don't know what to do when confronted. However you decide to deal with a bully, it should be done sooner rather than later.

Sometimes you gotta fight!

It may be a symbolic fight or a physical one, but there are times when you cannot avoid a fight. Try to avoid conflict, look for peaceful resolutions to problems, but recognize that there are times when strength and courage are required. Be brave.

Questions to Think About

- What are signs that something is troubling my child?

- Is there a known threat to me or my children's safety?

- Am I making healthy choices in front of my children?

- Can my children talk openly to me? Do I encourage them to come to me?

Final Thoughts

From this experience, I learned that you have to be tough-minded in order to survive in the world today. This story was about the moment I realized that I could be tough when I had to be. You might be minding your own business and people will go out of their way to mess with you. Have you ever felt like that?

If you are confident and know where you are headed, you will not let people stop you. Building that type of confidence in yourself takes time, but it is totally necessary. Sometimes you will face hard times and feel all alone. Keep pushing yourself forward – your reward is ahead of you. The next story is all about "pushing" past your problems.

CHAPTER 5

Push the Car

As a young, single mother of two kids, my mother was often embarrassed. She loved her children, but hated how the neighbors talked about us and our situation. We kept to ourselves a lot. After she earned her high school diploma, my mother made up her mind to better herself and go to college. She decided to sign up for a training program that she heard about.

One day she caught the bus downtown and went to sign up for a nursing program. She had all of her documents – her birth certificate, our birth certificates, driver's license, social security cards, etc. She knew from signing up for welfare that you had to bring all of your paperwork or the process could take forever. She arrived at the office and was given a clipboard of forms to fill out. The lobby was full of other women who were also signing up for the program. When she finished, my mother returned the clipboard to the receptionist. She stood there while the woman reviewed her documents.

"There's a problem," the receptionist said. My mother leaned in closer to see if she forgot to answer a question or needed more documentation. She got an answer when the receptionist said, in a loud voice, "You have 2 illegitimate children, the program is for mothers with one!"

My mother did not hear anything else the woman said after that. She gathered up her copies, slung her purse over her left shoulder and walked out of the office. She did not break down and cry until she was out of the building, away from the eyes of all the people she could feel looking at her. She lit a cigarette and got a tissue out of her purse. When she had cleared the tears from her eyes she looked across the street where they had recently built a new school - Cuyahoga Community College, the brown and tan building on the corner. She decided that since she was downtown anyway, why not see if she could sign up for school over there.

She entered the building and was wondering where she should go, when a nice woman walked over and asked if she needed help. My mother explained that she was interested in coming back to school to better herself. She was escorted to admissions and was given paperwork. When she finished the paperwork, she was sent over to the financial aid office, then to the career advisors office. She ended up spending several hours at the campus. When she left, she was officially enrolled in college! She had a school schedule and a voucher to pick up her textbooks.

Tri-C, as the school was called, was one of the first community colleges in the country. My mother would learn firsthand that it was a safe place, a haven for anyone who wanted a better life. She would earn an Associate's degree at Tri-C, making her the first person in our immediate family to graduate college.

A few months before graduating, my mother discovered that she was pregnant. She was working and going to school, and had managed to buy a used car. Her orange Chevy Nova took us everywhere - to school, the grocery store, and other important places. We were so happy to get a car! We would not need to beg people to drive us places anymore. It was hard for my mother to ask people to take her and two kids shopping or to the doctor's office. We took the bus when we could, but some places were just too far away. Anyway, that car was our lifeline.

One day the car started sputtering and cutting off. We prayed to get home safely. It was snowing and getting dark. My little sister was scared and my mother was lighting up a cigarette. We finally made it to our street and the car stopped outside our house, right in the middle of the street. It would not start back up, so my mother told us that we would have to push the car into our driveway.

My mother and I pushed the car, while my little sister tried to steer. We struggled in the snow. My fingers started getting cold and I was worrying about my mother. She was pregnant and probably shouldn't be pushing a car. At one point I looked at the house across the street and saw our neighbors looking at us. I hoped that somebody would come help, but I knew better. They wouldn't help us. They stood there in the window and laughed at us. I started to cry. We were trying so hard to push the car -- we only needed to get it out of the street and into our own driveway. We knew that if it was left on the street it would get towed, after it was stripped of anything valuable.

We had no choice. This car must get into this driveway. Immediately.

I can still remember how cold and lonely it felt. By now we were all crying, but we kept pushing. It seemed like hours passed by. I kept looking at the house next to us…if our neighbor, Dwight, was home, I knew he would help us. Dwight was kind. He always helped us. But I didn't see his car – he must be at work, I thought to myself.

We girls kept pushing and eventually moved the car into the driveway! We were so proud and happy. We did it! When we got inside my mother made hot chocolate. After we got settled down and my sister went to bed, my mother and I started thinking about how we could get the car fixed. We had to have transportation. She was too close to finishing school and our schedule was too hectic to go back to public transportation or asking for rides.

She pulled out her phone book and started making calls. Another single mother had a good mechanic that she recommended to us. He fixed our car for a fair price. My mother finished college that spring. She also gave birth to my little brother.

This story was about some of the many obstacles that my family faced. It reminded me how much I was involved in worrying about the household and our struggles from a very young age. Our adversity had at least one positive result – we bonded as a close-knit unit, facing each challenge together. We learned to ignore what people said about us, to our faces and behind our backs.

From *Pushing the Car* here is what I learned:

Lessons Learned

Big opportunities often come after failure

My mother was devastated when the nursing program did not work out. She could have gone home and given up hope. Instead she chose to look into a different opportunity and enrolled in college. If your Plan A doesn't work, dry your tears and look around for the next opportunity, it could work out even better than your original idea.

People can be cruel. Don't try to understand why, just keep moving your life forward

You will always encounter opposition when you try to do something with your life. You will meet people who are mean to you. You must not waste time trying to figure out why. You just need to learn how to identify who is for you and who is not. Accept the information once it is revealed to you.

Sometimes no help is coming, it's all on you... sometimes you got to push the car!

Things are always hard when you have limited resources. Resources might be people, money, or knowledge. For example, AAA is great for those times when your car breaks down. But what happens when you don't have a AAA card? Sometimes no help is available and it is all on you. You have to be prepared to push a few cars in your life.

Commit to moving yourself forward, despite the obstacles. Adversity builds your coping muscles. Work yourself toward having a credit card for emergencies or joining AAA. Think about building a network of people that you can truly count on. While you are doing so, also become the kind of person that others can depend on.

Questions to Think About

- Have you ever felt humiliation? What did you do next?

- Who can you count on when you need help? If you have no one, how can you start to build a network of support? Do you support anybody else?

- What do you do when faced with obstacles?

Final Thoughts

In this remembrance, my mother faced a big disappointment. She had no direction and was just looking for someone to show her some kindness. As she kept searching she found a wonderful experience in the form of our local community college. You will win if you do not quit. Learn that success is a marathon, not a sprint. You must stay focused, ignore what your critics say, and take action.

You must also tackle each and every obstacle that comes your way. Learn how to show grace under pressure.

In the next story, I share one time when my family faced hardships during the holiday season.

CHAPTER 6

Christmas

*H*olidays were always a little hard on us. We usually had no money and people did not want to be bothered with us. One time, my mother noticed one of our cousins rolling her eyes when we stopped by her house on a holiday. "*Here come three more mouths to feed,*" her face seemed to say. After that, we limited our visits and absolutely never ate while over there.

We felt the most isolated from the rest of the world on holidays.

There was one exception to our isolation. One place where we always felt welcomed and loved - at Ms. Tommie's house! Ms. Tommie was a neighbor from our old neighborhood; my mom was her babysitter at one time. She was a kind, humble woman who was like a mother to all of us. Ms. Tommie and her family moved away from E. 80th Street and bought a house on the northeast side of Cleveland, off of Lakeview Road. We would make the long drive from Kinsman to Lakeview nearly every holiday. Her face would light up when she saw the three of us on her front porch. She would hug and kiss each of us as we entered the living room. I knew that Ms. Tommie was a God-fearing woman, she talked a lot about church and Jesus. What I liked most about her was how she made my mother feel. At Ms. Tommie's house my mother would relax and laugh and listen to Ms. Tommie. My mother would share stories from work or her plans for life after she finished school. Ms. Tommie was very proud of my mother and encouraged her more than anyone else, even members of our own family.

Whether we shared sweet potato pie at Christmas, an Easter feast in the springtime, or ribs on the fourth of July, every meal and every visit to Ms. Tommie's house left us with a warm feeling inside. Ms. Tommie and her family gave us so much love and peace and what we probably needed most of all – acceptance. It is a wonderful feeling to have at least one place on this earth where you can be yourself, and you don't have to call first before coming over.

I remember one year after dinner at Ms. Tommie's house we returned home to a pretty depressing scene.

My mother was expecting a baby and she was close to graduating from college. We had very little money, but knew if we could just hang on, just a little longer, things would improve when she finished school. There was no money for presents that year. We put up a little artificial Christmas tree, a tiny little thing, with just a few lights.

My mother got an idea. We got back in the car and drove to the 24-hour drug store. She used $20 to buy paint-by-number sets for us. Those would be our Christmas presents that year. The really nice ones came with velvet designs and thick oil or acrylic paints. The designs were various themes - horses, log cabins, and some had pretty winter scenes. We bought a plastic bag full of these sets and headed back home.

It was after dark, around 10 pm when we got home. We put on our pajamas and plugged in the Christmas lights and spread out in front of our little tree while we painted the paint-by-number sets. Those sets gave us a chance to be creative while giving us clear instructions on how to create the finished product. That's what we needed as a family too -- instructions on how to make a better life for us.

We sat up all night – laughing and talking; dreaming about how life would change for us when my mother graduated in a few months. It was snowing outside, but we were warm and happy. We lined the pictures on display around the Christmas tree. We all fell asleep around 5:30 in the morning, tired after working so hard on our artwork.

That Christmas was my worst Christmas. But it was also my best Christmas. We had each other, we were painting beautiful "masterpieces" as we imagined a better life ahead. Our little family would welcome a beautiful little boy in a few short months. My mother would complete her degree. We all expected that everything would get better. In some ways, we were emotionally – at times – on the positive side of the number line.

From the events in the story *Christmas* here is what I learned:

Lessons Learned

Know the places where you are celebrated and stay connected

It is important to recognize the places where you are always welcomed. We often expect that place to be among family members, but it does not have to be. I have at times found more kindness and acceptance from non-related people than my own relatives. L-O-V-E is not spelled F-A-M-I-L-Y. Many times the people that we expect to welcome us…well, they just don't! Accept this and move on. Their reasons are their reasons. You must find the places and people that love you and accept you. They should also be people that *correct* you. I have heard Ms. Tommie whisper to my mother that she needed to settle down and stop having so many men in and out of our house. And she was right. Eventually my mother listened to this wisdom, but not before some very terrible things happened. People that love you will correct your bad behavior and poor choices. Stay connected to them. Listen to them.

Eat good food with people that you love

I always thought that Ms. Tommie was the best cook. I now realize that her cooking was fine, but what made everything taste so special was the love that surrounded her meals. For our young family, her meals -- shared with her own family -- provided us a sense of belonging, genuine care, and protection. At her table we were loved. At her table we were removed from the stress, financial pressure, and fear of the unknown that we always seemed to feel.

Be able to enjoy the simple things in life

The inexpensive little paint-by-number sets gave us hours of enjoyment that Christmas. I understand now that the paint sets did many things – they tapped into our creativity and focused our energy to complete a project together. Most important, they gave us a sense of hope. We created these beautiful pictures while living on welfare and sitting in an empty house. Your current situation is not your destiny. Quiet your fear, stress, and other demons. Relax your heart and find ways to enjoy simple things in a chaotic world.

Questions to Think About

- Are there any isolated people around you? Think of ways that you can reasonably help them to feel connected.

- Who knows your current situation but seems like they don't care? Why do they matter?

- What is your dream for the future?

Final Thoughts

These two memories – Ms. Tommie's house and my worst/best Christmas -- remain vivid in my head. I am grateful that we had one place where we felt comfortable. When you live in tough circumstances it is very easy to forget to be grateful for what you do have. What (or who) are you grateful for today?

God has often reminded me that I have what I need for this exact moment. The test is what do you do with what you have while you wait for better days ahead. You can choose to be bitter and angry; or you can choose to grow and reach for better. Our family always kept hoping and moving toward a better time ahead. That was the secret to our survival and it can deliver you out of bad situations.

CHAPTER 7

A New Years View

A week after we stayed up all night on Christmas Eve, we were getting ready for New Years' Eve. It was always so funny to me how before Christmas the air was so holy, the music so religious, and the quiet snowflakes looked so beautiful and clean. Then only a few days later the city got loud and the snow in the streets got dirty. Party people began drinking and partying their behinds off. Being on vacation gave me a chance to take all of this in. I loved the two week holiday break. By December in Cleveland, winter was in full swing and you could expect some heavy snow days. Being out of school allowed me time to stay at home, playing with my friends, or hanging out with my uncles.

One of my uncles owned a night club and was planning a big New Years' Eve party. He asked if I wanted to work with him and of course I said yes. He was my businessman uncle. He had a gift for opening all kinds of business ventures. I tagged along to help out with most of them. I never earned a lot of money, but always enjoyed the experience. I had just turned 13 a month earlier, and felt so grown-up helping out at his club.

My uncle is the main reason that I became an entrepreneur. My mother thought entrepreneurs were "flaky" - people who couldn't find real jobs. She tried hard to extinguish my entrepreneurial spirit, but never could. I would work "real" jobs, but I always longed for my own business. I think she secretly blamed her brother for influencing me so much.

The afternoon and evening of this particular New Years Eve we worked hard at the club getting ready for the doors to open. My uncle checked the sound equipment, and did a walk-thru to make sure that the place was clean. He inventoried the food and liquor. I watched him put his crew of employees to work, handing out tasks large and small. The club was located in East Cleveland on Euclid Avenue, and it was huge, it had 3 levels. There were big open spaces for dancing, and small private rooms to watch music videos and eat dinner. There was even a video game arcade on the lower level. There was truly something for everyone to do.

My job for the evening was to run the coat check room. My uncle's girlfriend, who also worked at the club, gave me quick training on what to do. The most important thing was to not lose anybody's coat or give the wrong coat to the wrong person. We had claim tickets and hangers for 200 coats. I was pretty organized and was sure that I could handle things.

There was such excitement in the air. Guests started rolling in and I could hear music and laughter from throughout the building. They were all dressed up and some of the ladies smelled so nice. I was very professional as I greeted the ladies and gentlemen. I was handed fur coats and floor length leather coats and fancy canes. Since the men were checking their canes with me, I guess they were for decoration and not really needed for mobility.

I was fascinated with the variety of people I saw. My uncle would greet the important people and he introduced me, too. He checked on me several times during the evening and even had one of the security guards bring a plate of food to me, since I could not leave my station. People started giving me tips as the evening went on. After we ran out of hangers, I quickly started a system of placing coats on empty chairs - alphabetically by last name. No coat would be misplaced on my watch.

I leaned on the counter of the little coat room and looked out at the crowd of guests. They seemed to be having the time of their lives. And they were spending lots of money. I was happy for my uncle. He was having a great night for his business. After the countdown to the new year, the champagne toasts and kisses, the party continued for a few more hours. I handed many coats over that counter to departing guests, one-by-one. They continued to give me tips, especially the ones who were intoxicated.

As the last few guests started leaving the night club, my uncle's girlfriend came over to get me. She would drive me home and return to meet my uncle after he closed up. I could not understand how people could stay up this late every weekend. I was exhausted.

The next morning was New Years Day and my mother would be taking me to work with her. She was a social worker at a community center and explained that I would be helping to feed the homeless. She would be working in her office catching up on paperwork while I was to work in the kitchen with the other volunteers. My mother insisted that we spend time volunteering. We must help others, she always taught us. We were never to forget that somebody out there was worse off than us and we had a responsibility to get involved. "Be the answer to someone else's problem," was her philosophy.

My job that day was to prepare the dining hall for the lunch meal and to help serve the food. I put plastic tablecloths on the long tables and set up folding chairs. As people started arriving, I was assigned a spot in the food line, passing out the bread – "only two slices per person," I had been instructed. After everyone had been fed, those who wanted seconds could go through the line again. I greeted everyone with a smile and many times heard, "God bless you" from the people getting a good hot meal.

Looking over the crowd of hungry citizens I saw a variety of people – single men, women and kids, young people and old people. Some had on work uniforms, while others were dressed in rags. I saw some people looking through the newspaper, in search of a job, I guessed. Some sat in groups and talked while others sat alone and stared blankly at the wall. It was cold that day and I could almost see people warming up as they ate. I wondered what they were thinking about as they enjoyed the meal.

The center was located on Detroit Avenue, on the lower west side of Cleveland, near the bridge. A group of very nice and friendly people from the church next door moved among the crowd, sharing the gospel with those who were willing to listen. After finishing their meals, people began putting on their coats, bundling up to return back outside into the cold.

After the meal was over, I helped to clean the dining hall – sweeping the floor, clearing dishes from the tables, folding the chairs and stacking them against the wall. We had to clean the place spotless because another meal would be served in a few hours. Most of those who were eating lunch would be back later that evening for dinner.

Riding home with my mother I was lost in my thoughts.

I saw two different views of life during that New Year's holiday. In the last 24 hours my same two hands had handed strangers their $5,000 fur coats and bread wrapped in aluminum foil. I witnessed people both dancing while sipping champagne and quietly drinking punch from Styrofoam cups. I wondered about all of these folks and their stories. How did they get to this point in their lives? I wondered.

rom the events in the story *A New Years View* here is what I learned:

Lessons Learned

Life is filled with differences – some people you meet will be wealthier than you, others will be poorer than you -- Notice them all

It was a good early lesson for me to spend time with both the party people and the homeless people over the same weekend. It helped me to stop comparing my situation to families who had more than us. I was reminded that some people had even less than we had. I began to understand that we must all make the best of what we have. I also thought about the Bible verse that says, "to whom much is given, much is required." How much you have is not just measured in dollars. My mother's determination to help others, in the face of her own troubles, was priceless.

Serving others is noble

When things are hard for us, it is easy to grow self-centered and selfish. Learning to step out of your "stuff" and serve others will often attract blessings to your situation. Nothing feels better than helping a person in need without expecting a thing in return from them. Doing good is a reward all by itself. Planting seeds of goodness will reap a harvest back onto you and your family!

Help out your entrepreneurial relatives or friends

We all have them or have seen them -- those energetic relatives or friends who are always "working on something big." There may be several "big" projects over the years. Please try to be supportive of them. Entrepreneurs are visionaries! They see connections that others do not see; they desire greatness that others do not think is possible. Deep down they know that many people do not approve of how they live (*"Why doesn't he just get a real job?"*). Most are truly hard working folks who dare to be different. They desperately need someone to believe in them. But if you cannot believe in them...at least do not discourage them. Who knows, one day maybe one of their projects will make it big.

Questions to Think About

- Do you treat people differently based on what they have? Why or why not?

- Who needs your unique talents, gifts, and abilities? Are you spending at least one hour each week helping this group?

- Are you living your best possible life? What would you change?

Final Thoughts

This was a fun recollection about my experience "people watching" during a New Years' holiday. I think that it stands out as a strong memory because for the first time I saw a contrast in economic status played out in front of me. The experience reminded me to be kind to all people. The most important lesson I learned was to commit my life to volunteer service. Volunteering is a great human experience that builds people, communities, and countries. These days many school systems require students to earn volunteer hours in order to graduate. Hopefully, we all will learn to carve out even small amounts of time for such a noble cause.

CHAPTER 8

Shoes

After the holiday break, I returned to school and had a pretty good second semester. I was asked to speak at my 6th grade graduation. I was used to speaking by then, after years of reciting poems, and acting as the young mistress of ceremony for various programs. I was well known at my elementary school for my gift of public speaking. As June approached I got nervous about what I would wear to graduation. My little brother was only a few weeks old and money was very tight around our house.

My mother requested a clothing voucher from her welfare caseworker. If that came through, maybe I could get a new outfit, and some shoes, too, to wear for graduation. I tried not to worry about it.

One day, as I was getting ready to leave school, my teacher called me over and handed me a sealed envelope to give to my mother. It was paperwork for my mother to return to our caseworker. My teacher had to verify that I was poor and needed a clothing voucher. Needing help always puts a lot of people in your business. You get used to it. I was just glad that the paperwork did not get lost like it usually does when something gets sent directly to the welfare office. That's why my mother asked that the teacher return it to her and she would hand deliver the papers to the caseworker.

The voucher got mailed to our house about a week later. My mother said that we would go shopping that Saturday. Graduation was next week, but I was trying not to get nervous.

When Saturday came my sister and I got dressed and we all headed out. We needed to go grocery shopping and then to the department stores to buy my graduation outfit. We had to go to two different stores because one voucher was for clothing and the other was for shoes. My mother was annoyed because that was going to use up a whole lot of gas. I stayed quiet while we drove around, I did not want to get on her nerves.

The department store was first. We tried several stores, but could not find anything. Finally, at Sears, we picked out a suit from the women's department because I was big for my age. It was a light grey two-piece with a jacket and skirt. I didn't like it very much. I told my mother that the school said we were supposed to wear blue or black and she told me that, "the school needed to buy it then." Translation: we would buy whatever we could find! She was getting more annoyed, so I just got quiet.

We went to the shoe store next. It was late in the afternoon and we were all tired. My mother had left the baby at home with my grandmother, who gave strict instructions, "don't be gone too long."

The shoe store was our last stop and it was very busy. When the clerk came over to help us my mother handed him the voucher. He said that he would have to get his manager to handle the paperwork. The manager was an older man who walked very slowly. He came out onto the showroom floor, looked over our voucher and told us to follow him as he walked back into the storeroom. "You can pick anything on this rack," he said and returned to his desk. The rack was full of men and women's shoes. They were all dusty and ugly. We tried to find my size, but it wasn't looking good. "Do you have any other sizes?" my mother asked the manager. "Just what's on the rack," he said. "Those are the only shoes you can buy with that voucher." I looked at my mother's face and saw a flash of sadness. We looked harder to find a pair of shoes for my graduation.

She picked up a pair of blue suede earth shoes and told me to try them on. They were my size. "But these don't match," I told her. "And they're ugly!" I added. My mother lost it. "If your foot wasn't so damn big, maybe we could find a pair that fit," she screamed at me. Other customers looked into the storeroom at us and the manager glanced over, too. "Let's just get these," I said quietly. My little sister, standing beside me, reached over and held my hand.

A week later I went to my sixth grade graduation. When I walked into school my teacher frowned and said that I was supposed to be wearing blue or black. She started to say something more, but didn't. I just looked at her but did not say a word. Nobody from my family could come that day, so I just wanted to give my speech and go home. I walked across the stage in a light grey suit and blue earth shoes; I gave an eloquent speech, received my certificate, and ended my elementary school education.

Who knows what middle school will be like, I thought to myself as I walked home, my feet hurting in my blue suede earth shoes.

From the events in the story *Shoes* here is what I learned:

Lessons Learned

Help people in a dignified manner

While I was very grateful that we were able to get assistance from the welfare department, it was a very demeaning experience. Being told to select from old, dusty, and unwanted items because we were paying with a voucher was traumatic for me and heartbreaking for my mother. Nobody WANTS to be in need, it just happens to some of us during seasons of our lives. Fortunately we were a strong and highly motivated family, but what happens to families who do not have the self-esteem and motivation that we had? I hope that our country learns to help people while allowing them to keep some self-respect.

Parents must find a way to redirect frustration

Inside the shoe store, my mother was screaming at her circumstances, not me. She was in pain from poverty and feeling overwhelmed with too many kids and too little money. It came out directed at me, but her frustration was bigger than a scene in a shoe store. I would encourage parents to manage their frustration. Aim it elsewhere --anywhere but toward your children. My mother did not even remember the incident years later, but I will never forget it. Remember that your children did not ask to be here. Once children are born, however, it is your job to raise them without doing too much damage. I say this because children do not come with instructions and parents have to experience on-the-job training. Be the parent that your child needs.

Be sensitive to seeing or hearing the suffering children around you

Most of my teachers were supportive of me. There were times, though, when an extra little patience and kindness would have helped me. I comprehended that we were *supposed* to wear blue or black to my graduation ceremony. I even communicated that information to my mother, at my own risk. I hope that with the changing demographics at public schools, teachers today are a lot more understanding of what some kids must endure at home.

Learn to forgive

I was wounded that day at the shoe store. When I travel to do presentations and recall the story, I still tear up. Every time. I literally make myself share the story because just maybe it will help a kid, or single parent, or father, whose absence has thrown his family into poverty. I survived this story and many others by learning the lesson, AND forgiving the person who inflicted the pain. We must all learn to forgive – ourselves, our parents, our decisions, etc. It is truly the only way that you can survive the past and work toward a better future.

Questions to Think About

- Do you have an upcoming financial need that is causing you stress? What are some proactive solutions?

- What are some creative ways to solve your current problem?

- How can you avoid this type of situation in the future?

- How can you push yourself through difficult times? What are some ways to stay motivated when the present seems dark?

Final Thoughts

This memory is painful and difficult to share. I had the opportunity to look at it in a different way recently. Someone pointed out that I remained respectful to my mother; clearly showing how much I loved her. I also went to school and gave my speech. The person pointed out that many kids would have stayed home and avoided an uncomfortable situation. Wow. I had never thought of it that way. Looking back, I have <u>always</u> faced difficult situations… head-on! The shoe store experience and many more like it, have shaped me into the person that I am today. All of the wounds, warts, and scars that I have collected along the way have created the story of my life.

The next chapter shares a story from my first year of middle school.

CHAPTER 9

Home

"How are things at home?" the school guidance counselor asked. We were nearly done discussing my schedule. I was placed in advanced classes, and was assigned to Home Economics as my elective. I was in her office because I wanted to transfer into the Shorthand and Typing program. When she asked me to explain my request, I shared that I could use typing to get an office job one day, but I really wasn't too interested in cooking.

She said that I was a little young to be thinking about a job and asked if I worried about money. I gave a short and untrue answer just to get out of her office. We were trained to keep people out of our business as much as possible.

"How are things at home?" I could hear her as I walked home, thinking to myself...let's see - my mother had just graduated college, had a baby and had recently married my second stepfather, who hated me. I know this because he

said so, all of the time. It was cool because I hated him, too. So home was a little tough, but it was going to get better.

This was my mother's second marriage. Being married was very important to my mother. My first stepfather had been nice enough. He was a good person. He always kept a job at least. He rode a motorcycle and loved music. Every payday he would take my mother to the music store to buy albums. They got along most of the time, except when he was drinking. She tried to hold the marriage together, but it only lasted a few years.

The first time I met stepfather #2 he wore white pants, and his hat tilted to the side. I disliked him instantly. This guy was going to be trouble. I could tell from the very beginning. All I knew about him was that they worked together. My mother had got her first real career job, after graduating from college earlier that year. He came into our lives when I was turning 13, my sister was 10, and our little brother was just a few months old. He had never been around kids and always seemed uncomfortable with us. At least he bonded with the baby.

I remember that my stepfather always liked to dress. When they met, he lived in the projects down on Cedar. It was a rough neighborhood at the time; thieves kept breaking in his apartment. That happened twice and they stole his clothes and other stuff. The next thing I know he asked my mother to marry him. He would be moving into the two-family house with us. I always believed that he married my mother just to get out of the projects and move uptown where we lived. I could be wrong.

They argued all the time. Over the course of their 10-year marriage he moved in and out so many times -- more than I can count. He would leave in the springtime, but before winter he always seemed to reconcile with my mother and move back in.

My mother always explained to us that she was just trying to make a family. Before each marriage she sat us down and gave us this message.

I wished that I could explain to her that we were already a family. We had our own house and these guys did not. Both had moved in with us! Between marriages my mother kept moving men into our home. Even as a child I knew that this was not good. It was not safe. Sometimes she let monsters in...

Home holds our hopes and dreams. It is the "headquarters" for the family – missions are planned and resources are managed inside the home. When she was man-less, my mother understood this and we would grow as a family. Our finances, education, even our spirituality was strong...until she needed a man around. Companionship is a human need. That was not the problem. Choosing the wrong men was the problem. That can be dangerous for everyone.

We were damaged in many ways because of allowing monsters into our home. It was during those middle school years that home was stressful, depressing, and often filled with violence and abuse. My school guidance counselor had no idea what I was living with at home. And she would never hear about it from me.

In spite of it all, we kept working hard toward building a better life for the family. I watched my mother find peace and self-esteem as she completed her undergraduate degree at Cleveland State University on Euclid Avenue. She suddenly became a working professional. A few years later, after I was in high school, she started thinking about maybe going back to school…again.

From the events in the story *Home* here is what I learned:

Lessons Learned

Parents have a responsibility to keep their children safe

Parenting is a demanding responsibility. You cannot afford to be lax. A mistake in judgment can cause life altering consequences for you and your children. I know parents who live with the deep guilt of having been careless and as a result compromised their kids' safety. Anything can happen, even when you are being a good and loving parent. I heard a story a few years ago about a little boy who begged his parents to let him walk to school by himself. They finally gave in and granted him his wish. The one and only time he ever walked himself to school he was abducted and killed. This is an extreme example, but my point is that anything can happen. Practice being on your game when it comes to being a parent. Don't take shortcuts, or cut corners unless you are willing to live with a bad outcome if something happens. Sometimes you, the parent, must make executive decisions when your kids want something that may be unsafe for them.

Everyone is not worthy to be in and around your house

Your household is not a bus station! You cannot take in the world's problems when you have children and other vulnerable family members under your roof. Everyone is not worthy to be in and around your house with free access. We are living in a time where identity theft and multiple forms of abuse are taking place right under our noses. Now don't get me wrong, I was raised to care for people. You must, however, gauge the most appropriate way to do so!

For some people, there is a reason why they cannot find anywhere to live, or why they are not welcome in certain places. Statistics estimate that one in four girls and one in six boys are sexually abused as children. I personally think that these numbers are grossly under reporting the truth. Also, in most cases, children are harmed by an adult who is known to them. You absolutely cannot have a lot of people running in and out of your home.

Stop lying to yourself. We convince ourselves that we are just doing our civic duty, being a good Christian, being a good neighbor, etc. That is called self-deception. If what you really need is companionship, sex, or money, be honest about it and find safer ways to accomplish this than bringing everybody into your house.

Every family needs to have a clear vision for the future

On a more positive note, every family needs a vision for the future. Families need to learn how to set goals. We need to have a clear vision for our collective futures. In my family, we always knew that once my mother graduated from college, we would all benefit. We set other goals, too. As we set and accomplished each goal, we grew closer as a family. We also grew stronger as people and learned to believe in the power of our family.

Questions

- Are you involved in healthy relationships?

- Who has access to your children? Are these people safe to have around? How do you know?

- Is there anybody in your household that maybe should not be there? What are your reasons for your answer?

- Have you set some goals for your family? What are they? Think about both individual members and the household as a whole.

Final Thoughts

In this chapter I shared the dark years of middle school and life with one of my stepfathers. Although in her mind my mother was trying to build a family, her romantic choices put us all in jeopardy. In the background of it all I tried to remember that "home" really symbolizes a safe place for its members.

The final story in the book talks about how this period of my life ended, when I graduated high school, and my mother completed graduate school.

CHAPTER 10

A Mother's Story

One secret to leveling the economic playing field in America is education. Our family was on welfare during my entire childhood. While on welfare, though, my mother kept going to school! She kept reaching for a better life for the family. She also pushed her children to do well in school. I began this book talking about starting life at -20. I was actually lucky. My parent's beginnings were much worse. Education can help you reach the positive side of the number line much faster. Education can be expensive but it is a good investment if you look at the long view and have a plan.

My mother decided to add graduate school to her plan. Graduate school was a very important season in her life. Before applying to grad school, she explained that with an advanced degree she could get a much better job after graduation. She had worked in the field of social work for a few years now and had gone as far as she could without more education. Her program would take eighteen months to finish. So here was one more mountain for the family to climb together until we reached the top.

During this time, my sister and I were both teenagers and our little brother was 7-years-old. We watched our mother juggle work, school, and a failing marriage. Fortunately she was highly motivated, intelligent, and driven. Most important of all she was loyal to her kids. In all honesty, I had watched my mother grow-up. It is a hard thing for a parent to have to grow up in front of their kids. All of your mistakes are played out in front of little watching eyes. All she needed was time -- time to grow-up and to mature. It's like the Bible says, God "made everything beautiful in its time."

While my mother was taking classes in graduate school we all helped out – I would type her papers, and my sister would take care of our little brother. We spent many weekends at the library working on research projects. We all became more disciplined and focused while "we" attended grad school. My mother believed in studying hard in order to thoroughly learn her craft. She took pride in being strong in both street knowledge and book knowledge.

After a long eighteen months my mother finally finished the coursework and announced her graduation day. My stepfather was acting funny in the days leading up to her graduation. He had a real attitude. Finally he told her that he was not going to her graduation. I was a senior in high school and about to graduate myself, so I knew that his decision stung her. Fortunately, I was able to stay home from school that day so that I could attend my mother's graduation.

Many years later, after they divorced, he would admit that his jealousy kept him from going to her graduation and he asked for her forgiveness. But his presence or absence did not matter; as always her kids were there for her and shared in her success. We were so proud of my mother.

The day of her graduation was a warm, sunny day. The students marched across Euclid Avenue with such pride and joy. Purple and yellow balloons were released and slowly floated up to the bright sunny sky. We took a picture of my mom in her cap and gown. I had never seen her look happier!

My mother was 36-years-old when she graduated with a Master's degree in Social Service Administration from Case Western Reserve University. She was now trained to design and run non-profit programs that would help people. Even though she was a "welfare mother" my mother had earned three college degrees while raising a family on food stamps. This final degree was quite an accomplishment, something special and very important. She was on her way professionally!

After being kicked out of public school because she was a pregnant, unwed mother, this remarkable woman never stopped pursuing a better life for herself and her kids. We had bumps along the way, and some poor decisions were made, but life was looking up for us and a happy ending was in sight. Her greatest accomplishment (according to her) was raising her children to become good people. Society wanted her to be ashamed of us, of how we got here and our illegitimacy. She did not listen to society. She took terrible, depressing, dangerous soil, and grew three beautiful flowers.

My mother inspired us with her creativity, sheltered us with her protection, and made us strong. She also taught us to care about other people.

Not only did my mother reach the positive side of the number line in her lifetime, she went much further than anyone ever expected her to go. She survived molestation, rape, and raising kids mostly alone in an urban environment and much, much more. Along the way she positively touched the lives of hurting people.

She would go on in her professional life to meet judges, Congressmen, two U.S. Presidents, and the Dalai Lama. She would write a book of poetry, teach college courses at her beloved Tri-C, and as a social worker help hundreds of clients overcome their addiction to alcohol and drugs. My mother's life was filled with tragedy and triumph, but she always embraced her story.

From the events in *A Mother's Story* here is what I learned:

Lessons Learned

Never stop reaching for more

As we lived our lives during those difficult years we never stopped reaching for more, for better. Thoughts of the future kept us going. My mother wrote a poem to her children called "Wings of Freedom." "Tomorrow is your sacred armor against the hopelessness of today," she wrote to us. You cannot allow yourself the luxury of giving up. And the worse your situation, the stronger your determination must be. The more obstacles that you face, the more focused you must remain. As you keep reaching, God rewards you with everything that you need.

Do not let negative people in your life stop your dreams

Negative people are dangerous. People who are jealous of you are equally dangerous. It is best to keep both kinds of people out of your life, but if they are around you, you cannot let them stop you. Be very careful of who you listen to. Find people who feed your confidence and creativity. Find people who you can talk to about yourself and your mess. Make sure that these people have your best interest in mind, really care about you. I believe that many dreams are killed because we share our ideas with the wrong people.

Your critics should have one purpose – to inspire you

Along with identifying any negative people in your life, you must also recognize your critics. We all have some people who are busy watching everything that we do and offering their comments. Ignore them. Keep devoting your time to building your dreams. Be inspired by your critics. Try not to be too disappointed when your critics are people who should be your supporters (like family members). I have learned that people can only give you what they have inside. How can someone nurture you if no one has ever nurtured them? Some people are just bitter, nasty, mean, and petty. Do your own thing while they keep watching. And one final tip. -- when you succeed -- these are often the first people who try to take the credit for your success! Statements, such as, *"I always knew that girl had it in her,"* or *"I was hard on him cause I knew he would be somebody one day!"* is what you will hear from insincere people on the other side of your story. You just stay focused and keep building, even if it takes years.

Became competent in your craft

My mother's graduate school experience taught me the importance of really learning your craft. She approached every project, class assignment, or term paper with fierce determination. She always went above and beyond expectations. The result was that when she graduated, she was sharp! She was knowledgeable and had real world experience. Too often we do not approach schoolwork with the understanding that it is preparing you for the world of work. Sloppy work habits can be traced back to sloppy school habits. We must learn how to get organized, how to study, how to ask questions, and how to pace ourselves when faced with a big project.

Questions

- How could your current family situation be improved?

- What lessons are people learning as they watch you?

- Who are the people who celebrate the important events in your life?

Final Thoughts

This final chapter focused on a major accomplishment in our family, one that moved our family financially to the positive side of the number line. After finishing graduate school, my mother's income doubled and she was finally able to provide for herself and her kids. We had beaten the odds! Our family was not another statistic on welfare anymore.

As I mentioned above, my mother wrote "Wings of Freedom" for her children. In it she says "*tomorrow is your sacred armor against the hopelessness of today.*" Amen to that. I hope that our story inspires anyone who may be experiencing a tough today…your story is not yet over. Keep striving.

CONCLUSION

Thank you for taking this journey with me and listening to my stories. Did you hear any words of wisdom that inspired you along the way? I have been open and honest with you about what happened, how it made me feel, or how I responded. I had the benefit of telling you my stories long after the events occurred. This is important because it allowed me to extract the important lessons to share with you.

Thankfully, my family survived and experienced happy endings.

You and your family can overcome challenges, too. I want to stay connected and show you how to focus and grow. Soon after I completed this project, I began working on two companion books that may interest you.

Do you have stories to share? Would you like to write a book? *Embracing My Story: A Story Starter Journal* will help you identify important stories from your life and write them. I will teach you how to do it. The journal offers step-by-step instructions about launching your own collection of stories. I will also help you to get the book published just like I did.

Maybe writing a book does not interest you. If you enjoyed the life lessons that I shared with you and want to continue working on yourself...think about my other companion book. *Building My Story: A Personal Growth Workbook* is a blueprint of practical strategies for improving your life. I discuss how to think about your life and family situation long term. As you discovered in this book, my family struggled for years to pull ourselves out of poverty and hopelessness. We did this by thinking strategically, making some power moves, and avoiding some dangerous roads along the way. I can show you how to do the same thing in your life!

You will find my contact information at the back of the book. May you accomplish every goal that you set.

Alisa Smedley

ABOUT THE AUTHOR

Alisa Smedley is an author, trainer, entrepreneur and subject matter expert in the field of reentry after incarceration. She believes that faith, hard work and optimism are all secrets to overcoming hardship. She is the owner of *Coach Smedley's Training Center*, a consulting practice that trains correctional educators and reentry practitioners. Her interests include military history, reading and dreaming. Smedley lives in Montgomery County, Maryland.

CPSIA information can be obtained
at www.ICGtesting.com
Printed in the USA
FSHW022352160521
81498FS

9 781953 755506